Butterflies

By Eric Braun and Sandra Donovan

Steadwell Books

Raintree Steck-Vaughn Publishers

A Harcourt Company

Austin · New York
www.steck-vaughn.com

ANIMALS OF THE RAIN FOREST

Published by Raintree Steck-Vaughn Publishers,
an imprint of Steck-Vaughn Company.

Library of Congress Cataloging-in-Publication Data
Braun, Eric, 1971-
    Butterflies/Eric Braun, Sandra Donovan.
        p.cm.—(Animals of the rain forest)
    Includes bibliographical references (p.31) and index.
    Summary: Describes the habitat, physical characteristics, and life cycle of
butterflies, most of whom live in tropical areas.
    ISBN 0-7398-4680-9
    1. Butterflies—Juvenile literature. [1. Butterflies. 2. Rain forest animals.] I. Title
II. Series: Animals of the rain forest.
QL544.2 .B68 2001
595.78'9—dc21

2001019829

Printed and bound in the United States of America
1 2 3 4 5 6 7 8 9 10 WZ 05 04 03 02 01

Produced by Compass Books

Photo Acknowledgments
Digital Stock, 28-29. Photo Network/Kevin Caldwell, title page; Ahmad M. Abdalla, 15;
Richard Cummings, 6. Root Resources/C. Postmus, 8, 20 (all photos on page); Earl L.
Kubis, 19, 26 (right). Tony Rath Photography, 16, 22. Visuals Unlimited/A. Kerstitch, 11;
Bill Beatty, 12; Fritz Pölking, 24; Kjell Sandved, cover, 26 (left).

Content Consultants
Cynthia Sims Parr, Content Development Director
Animal Diversity Web, University of Michigan Museum of Zoology

Maria Kent Rowell, Science Consultant, Sebastopol, California

David Larwa, National Science Education Consultant
Educational Training Services, Brighton, Michigan

This book supports the National Science Standards.

Contents

MEXICO

BELIZE
HONDURAS
NICARAGUA
GUATEMALA
EL SALVADOR
*Caribbean
Sea*

COSTA RICA

PANAMA

ECUADOR

COLOMBIA

VENEZUELA

GUYANA
SURINAME

*North
Atlantic
Ocean*

FRENCH
GUIANA
(FRANCE)

PERU

AMAZON
RIVER

BRAZIL

BOLIVIA

*South
Pacific
Ocean*

CHILE

PARAGUAY

*South
Atlantic
Ocean*

ARGENTINA

URUGUAY

Range of the
Blue Morpho
Butterfly

Surrounding
Land

Water

Borders

Rivers

N
W E
S

4

A Quick Look at Butterflies

What do butterflies look like?

Butterflies are many different colors and sizes. Their wings have different colors and markings. They have four wings, two on each side of their bodies.

Where do butterflies live?

Butterflies live all over the world, except near the North or South Poles. Most live in tropical places. The rain forests of Central and South America have more kinds of butterflies than anywhere else.

What do butterflies eat?

Butterflies eat only liquids. Usually, they eat nectar. Nectar is a sweet liquid found in plants and flowers. Some also feed on the juices of animals and waste. Many butterflies do not have to drink water. They get enough liquid from the nectar they drink.

Unlike other insects, butterflies taste
and smell with their feet.

Butterflies in Rain Forests

M any insects, such as dragonflies, have lived on Earth for 300 million years. The first butterflies only appeared about 120 million years ago. One scientific name for butterflies is Lepidoptera (lep-uh-DOP-tur-uh). The name comes from words that describe a butterfly's wings.

Butterflies are insects, like ants and beetles. An insect is an animal that has six legs and a body that is divided into three parts. The parts are the head, **thorax**, and **abdomen**. The thorax is between the head and the abdomen. The stomach is in the abdomen. Most insects also have wings.

▲ This caterpillar will undergo metamorphosis to turn into a butterfly.

Metamorphosis

Butterflies do not start as butterflies. First, they are **caterpillars**. Caterpillars look like worms. They have soft bodies and short, stumpy legs. They do not have wings.

After several weeks or months, caterpillars start to change into butterflies. This change is called **metamorphosis** (met-uh-MOR-fuh-siss).

Do some places have more butterfly species than others? Yes, they do. The small country of Costa Rica in Central America has many different kinds of butterflies. In fact, it has more butterfly species than all of Africa. What is a species? It is a group of animals or plants most closely related to each other.

Role in the Rain Forest

Butterflies have an important job in the rain forest. As they fly from one flowering plant to another, they brush against pollen on the plants. Pollen is a powdery material that plants make so new plants can grow.

Butterflies **pollinate**, or spread pollen, each time they visit a flower. By pollinating plants, butterflies make more plants grow. Without butterflies, there would be fewer flowering plants. Without flowering plants, there would be fewer butterflies.

Kinds of Rain Forest Butterflies

There are more than 28,000 different species of butterfly. A species is a group of animals or plants most closely related to each other. Most butterflies live in tropical places. These are hot and rainy areas of the world. Many are found in rain forests. Rain forests are warm places where a lot of rain falls. Many different kinds of trees and plants grow close together there.

Butterflies come in many different colors. Ulysses butterflies have bright blue wings. They live in the rain forests of Australia. They are sometimes called mountain blue butterflies. Zebra butterflies have yellow stripes on black backgrounds. They live in the rain forests of Central and South America.

Butterflies also come in different sizes. Some have a wingspan as large as a dinner plate. An animal's wingspan is the distance between the tips of its wings. One kind of butterfly called the Queen Alexandra's birdwing butterfly has a wingspan of more than 11 inches (280mm). The smallest butterfly is the western pygmy blue. Its wingspan is only 0.5 inch (15 mm).

▲ **This long-winged zebra butterfly is looking for food in a flower.**

Some butterflies fly very fast, and others are very slow. Monarch butterflies fly up to 17 miles per hour (27 km/hr) over long distances. Skipper butterflies are even faster, flying up to 30 miles per hour (48 km/hr). They cannot, however, fly very far at this speed. When they fly, they start and stop, start and stop, and start and stop, over and over.

These butterflies are puddling. They are drinking water from wet sand.

Where Butterflies Live

Butterflies live all over the world, except near the North and South Poles. They live where they can find the best climate and food to stay healthy. They also live where they are safest. The tropical rain forests of Central and South America have the most kinds of butterflies.

Butterflies use plants for shelter from the weather and also to hide from predators. Predators are animals that hunt other animals and eat them. The safest places for butterflies to sleep are under leaves or between cracks in rocks.

Groups of butterflies often rest in sunny spots. They need the heat and energy from the sun to warm their bodies. Their bodies must be warm to be able to fly. Some butterflies will spread their wings to soak up the sun's heat. This is called basking.

Groups of butterflies will also gather at wet or muddy spots on the ground. This is called puddling. They drink the water at these spots.

Many butterflies spend their whole lives in one place. Others travel great distances. They move with the seasons to find the best food and weather. This kind of travel is called migration.

Monarch butterflies migrate the farthest. In the fall, large groups of monarchs fly from North America to Central and South America. They have also been found in Australia, Hawaii, and on other islands in the Pacific Ocean.

Appearance

A butterfly's head includes its eyes and its **proboscis**. The proboscis is a part of the mouth. When it is not being used, the proboscis is rolled up under the butterfly's head. The head also has **antennae**, or feelers. Butterflies use their antennae to smell and to keep their balance when they fly.

Butterflies have four wings, two on each side of their thorax. Each species has different wing colors and markings. Some butterflies have colors that blend in with their habitat. A habitat is a place where an animal or plant usually lives. Shapes, patterns, and colors that help things blend into the background are called camouflage.

Kinds of Wings

The monarch's wings are bright orange with black lines and borders. This helps predators, such as birds and lizards, tell monarchs from other species. They leave monarchs alone because they taste bad.

Morpho butterflies have large blue wings. The undersides of their wings have spots. The spots look like eyes. They are called eye spots, and they fool predators. A bird aims for a butterfly's

▲ **The spots on the underside of this Morpho butterfly's wings protect it.**

head. If it is fooled by the eye spots, it strikes the butterfly's wings instead. This usually does not hurt the butterfly, and the butterfly escapes.

When a butterfly with large eye spots spreads its wings, it can look like a predator itself. One butterfly with large eye spots is the owl butterfly. When it spreads its wings, the eye spots look like an owl's eyes.

This butterfly is drinking nectar from the flower.

What Butterflies Eat

Caterpillars and butterflies eat different kinds of foods. Caterpillars eat small parts of plants, such as leaves. They have hard mouth parts for eating tough plant leaves. Caterpillars need to eat plants to grow into butterflies.

Once caterpillars change into butterflies, they do not eat any solid food. They only need liquid food, such as nectar. Nectar is a sweet liquid found in plants. Usually, butterflies eat only nectar from flowers. Some butterflies, however, also feed on the juices of dead animals and waste. Many butterflies do not have to drink water. They get enough liquid from the nectar they drink.

How Butterflies Eat

Because butterflies do not eat solid food, they never need to bite or chew. Most insects have jaws, but butterflies do not. Instead, they use their proboscis. The proboscis works like a straw to suck up liquid food. Butterflies unroll their proboscis and poke it deep into flowers to find nectar. Then they suck up the nectar. Butterflies have a special pump in their bodies called a cybarial pump. This pump helps them suck.

How Butterflies Find Food

The first thing many caterpillars eat is the egg case from which they hatch. Usually, caterpillars hatch right on the plants that will be their food. They use their short legs to climb around the plant to eat small parts of the leaves.

Caterpillars eat to stay healthy and to change into butterflies. Once they become butterflies and have wings, they fly from plant to plant to find food.

Butterflies can see well, and this helps them find food. They can see the bright colors of flowers. They can also see some colors that people cannot see. These colors show butterflies where nectar is.

▲ This butterfly has its proboscis rolled up under its head.

A butterfly's feet also help it find food. When it lands on a plant or flower, its feet can sense wetness. This tells the butterfly if the plant has nectar to eat. Butterflies have a very good sense of smell. They smell through their feet and their antennae. Their sense of smell also helps them find flowers with nectar.

The Metamorphosis of a Butterfly

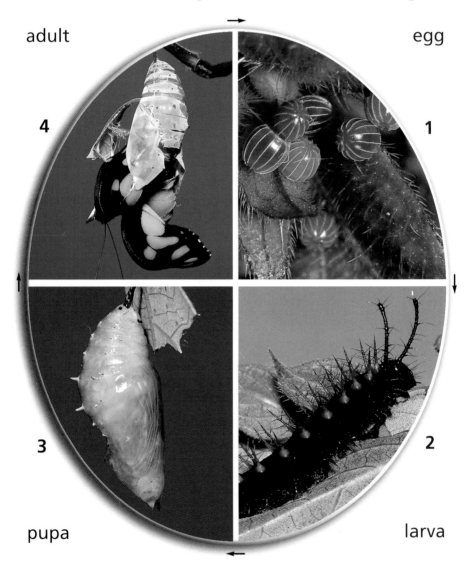

adult

egg

4

1

pupa

larva

3

2

A Butterfly's Life Cycle

B utterflies pass through four stages in their lives. The stages are the egg, the **larva,** or caterpillar, the **pupa**, and the **adult,** or butterfly.

Butterfly eggs hatch into caterpillars. Caterpillars have a head, a thorax, and an abdomen. They have 13 body sections and several legs. All caterpillars can spin silk threads.

Caterpillars crawl around eating leaves and growing larger. They molt, or shed their old skin for new skin, as they grow. After a few weeks, they attach themselves to a leaf or a branch. They molt one last time. This time, under the old skin is a chrysalis or a cocoon. It becomes hard. Inside the chrysalis, the caterpillar becomes a pupa.

The pupa goes through a process called metamorphosis. Metamorphosis means a change in form.

This butterfly is crawling out of its chrysalis.

Pupa to Adult

The pupa changes into an adult butterfly. It grows legs, wings, and antennae. The change may take from a few days to two years.

After metamorphosis, the skin of the pupa splits open. Then the adult butterfly crawls out. After only a few hours, it is ready to fly away. Most butterflies only live for a few days or weeks. Because their life is short, they look for a mate right away.

Usually, males travel in groups to look for females. Sometimes they gather on one plant and wait.

Butterflies only mate with butterflies of the same species. They use their good sense of sight to see colors and patterns on other butterflies. This helps them tell if another butterfly is the same species.

Butterflies also use their sense of smell to find mates. Females have a special scent that attracts males. Males will sometimes follow a scent for long distances. Once a male finds a female, he releases a scent, too. It usually comes from his wings or abdomen.

Laying Eggs

Female butterflies usually lay their eggs in the summer soon after mating. Butterflies usually lay eggs on the underside of plant leaves. The eggs are often colored to blend in with the leaves.

Females usually lay many eggs at once. This is because a lot of the eggs will be eaten by other animals before they can hatch. The more eggs a female lays, the better the chance of hatching.

Butterflies need rain forest trees and plants to live in. They can die without their habitat.

How Are Butterflies Doing?

There are not as many butterflies now as there were only a few years ago. More than 20 species of butterflies are endangered just in the United States. Endangered means all of a species could die out if things are not done to protect them and their habitats.

People are the biggest danger to butterflies. People are cutting down trees in the rain forests to build roads and buildings. They are clearing land for crops and animals. They are also selling the wood from the trees. Many animals in the rain forests, including butterflies, are losing their habitat.

Butterfly

Moth

Do you know some of the differences between a butterfly and a moth?

When do they fly?

Most butterflies fly during the day.

Most moths fly at night.

Do they look the same?

Butterflies are usually brightly colored.

Moths usually have dull colors.

Are their antennae alike?

Butterflies have knobbed antennae that look like clubs.

Moths have antennae that are often straight, feathery, or branched.

What happens to their wings when they rest?

Butterflies usually fold their wings together.

Moths rest with their wings open.

Future of Butterflies

Some people collect butterflies. Hunters capture and kill butterflies, and then sell them. Collectors display the dead butterflies for other people to see.

Butterflies are also having a harder time finding host plants. Host plants are plants that butterflies need for food, for places to sleep, and for laying eggs. These plants live in the rain forests that are being destroyed.

Some people are trying to save butterflies. They work to save their homes and host plants. They try to teach others about how important butterflies are to flowering plants. These people know that learning about butterflies is one of the best ways to save them. Together, people can use what they learn to help keep butterflies alive in their rain forest homes.

antennae
see page 19

proboscis
see page 14, 18

legs and feet
see page 19

colorful wings
see page 14

abdomen
see page 7

Glossary

abdomen (AB-duh-muhn)—the back part of an insect's body

adult (uh-DUHLT)—the final stage of an insect's development, such as a butterfly

antennae (an-TEN-ee)—feelers on the head of an insect

caterpillar (KAT-ur-pil-ur)—the worm-like larva stage in a butterfly's life cycle

larva (LAR-vuh)—an early stage of an insect's development, such as the caterpillar stage in a butterfly's life cycle

metamorphosis (met-uh-MOR-fuh-siss)—changes in an insect, such as a butterfly, as it develops from an egg into an adult

pollinate (POL-uh-nate)—to spread pollen so that new plants can grow

proboscis (pruh-BAH-sis)—a straw-like body part animals use to suck up liquids

pupa (PYOO-puh)—the stage of an insect's development just before it becomes an adult

thorax (THOR-aks)—the middle part of an insect's body between its head and abdomen

Internet Sites

The Butterfly Website
http://butterflywebsite.com

USGS Children's Butterfly Site
http://www.mesc.nbs.gov/butterfly/Butterfly.html

Useful Address

International Federation of Butterfly Enthusiasts
109 Sundown Court
Chehalis, WA 98532

Books to Read

Crewe, Sabrina. *The Butterfly.* Austin, TX: Raintree Steck-Vaughn Publishers, 1997.

Shaw, Nancy J. *Butterfly.* Mankato, MN: Creative Education, 1998.

Index